America On Lies

To order additional copies, please contact us.
BookSurge, LLC
www.booksurge.com
1-866-308-6235
orders@booksurge.com

America On Lies

America On Line Owns Americaonlies.com And .net. Don't Let Them Brain Wash You Or Your Children Any More. Go To Americaonlies.org For The Truth.

Mark Cullin

2006

America On Lies

AMERICA ON LIES

2-3-06. I wasn't going to do this but I have become completely disgusted with this, so called, America On Line. For most of you who would rather "Surf", P.S. Whatever the hell that means, the web, watch Hella Vision, play with your cell phone, I-pod, MP-3, X-box, Playstation-2 and what ever other garbage that's distracting you from your existence, I'll get right to the point. America On Line, "Owns", AMERICA ON LIES. COM, and, AMERICA ON LIES .NET. I'll spell it out for you internet junkies. americaonlies.com and americaonlies.net. Guess they don't want the truth getting out there ha??? Who are they, one corporation, claiming to be a nation on line? Don't let them, America on Line, AOL, brain wash you or your children no more. It is worse than Drugs this addiction called the personal computer. Oh and by the way, forgive me for all my grammatical errors. I need a spelling and english refresher course. Normal social interaction has declined tremendously since the internet revolution. I think I mention this in the pages ahead but just in case I don't, here it goes again. Its not only America online, it is the whole computer concept. Like television. We keep looking into it, yet we get nothing in return. One big Lie. It mentally stimulates us, however we do not get the physical and emotional interaction we crave and need so bad as human beings. Now get this and pay attention. "That's why we keep going back for more". It is a psychosis that plays on our mind, spirit and emotions. You will never get the fulfillment that you need and crave staring at an illusion that they call the computer monitor. They got you good these big internet companies. Serving up one big lie after the other. Keep you in a brain dead mesmerized state so you keep coming back for more. I just bought AMERICAON-LIES.ORG, laymens terms,americaonlies.org. It's time for some one to give them a run for their money. I don't give a hoot about money, P.S. Probably why I am broke. "I just want the truth to be told". So go to americaonlies. org and hopefully I can save a few people from this plague, AOL. As I get ready to send this book to the publisher America on line is sending out all those pop ups that keep poisoning your mind. Amazing! This one I see says, What men want for valentines day. Who are they to tell America what men want for valentines day? All materialistic stuff so woman can go buy it for them. Maybe men want something emotional. Like some appreciation from some of you ladies out there. I won't mention any names, you women know exactly who you are. And the other ladies get my point. Heres another pop up, "Britney busted with baby on lap". Who gives a crap about her. She stole another man's wife. And they give her publicity. Just like the guy who is the daddy. He supposedly already cheated on here. Noooo, I can't believe it. I thought he was a stand up kind of guy. What a joke. This is the information they are force feeding America every second of time.

The garbage that kids, young adults, and adults are exposed to on here is demonic and exasperating. P.S. Whatever that means. Its not just America On Line, it's everything and everywhere. "Ungodliness" surrounds this nation that is fixated on immorality as a whole. Its time for the American people to know the truth whether President Bush exports me to Iraq or not. I need to add this, remember how the gas prices shot up almost a full dollar after the Hurricane in New Orleans? Of course you do. Then the government had all the oil executives "ordered" to federal court. I would say "supenid" but I am not sure how to spell that word. There all sleeping in the same bed any way but they wanted us "Americans" to think they were looking out for us. As you recall the gas prices quickly shot back down almost a full dollar. But as time went by we forget so easily and prices started climbing back up again. P.S. Do any of you reading these words happen to have Jesus Christs' toll free phone number by any chance????? Some one has got to give this guy a call. Don't worry, I will know what to tell him. You just leave it to me and I will let him know what the deal is down here in America.

It's amazing how just one guy gets to speak and take action for a whole country, "America". No need to go there though, a lot of different opinions on that war of "His" that has been going on for several years now. Now I know why I have been procrastinating getting this book published "America On Lies". Obviously there was some information missing.

Super Bowl Sunday weekend. Here's one big "Lie" right here. Who gives a Shit? Apparently a lot of stupid Americans who are being deceived by the Media, Corporations, Professional sports teams, P.S. I use the word,

"Professional" lightly here and who ever else can make money out here off us idiots who waste our time attending and watching these over paid crybabies. The big talk on America on line and hella vision, "The news", is the $2.5 million dollar commercial spots for 30 seconds. Great deal ha? Jessica Simpson walking into your living room dressed like a stripper carrying a Pizza pie. Do us Moron men actually think that if we call Domino's and order up a Large pie with meatballs, That this Exhibitionist is going to deliver it to our front door??????? Give me a break. It's all about Sex in this country. How bout them there beer commercials. That woman prancing through the bar with a cold frosty one right in her hand doesn't even drink soda let alone beer. Boy she looks good don't she guy's?? Guess what fellas?? You ain't get any of her either, after you go buy that beer she got in her hand. She stirred your imagination and attention though. Job well done by the corporation to sucker you into buying their product. It's sad they all have to use sexism to sell the crap they are serving up to you and I. Well I ain't buying into it any more and neither should you. Sexual immorality, Every where you look. Sodom and Gomorrah was like this as well many years ago. Go buy yourself a bible and find out what God did to them people. Read, "The Death of America" while you're at it as well. Plain and simple and a very short book. "No God" "No Good", period. If this book don't get me sent to the Klinker, then I am sure that one will.

Anyway, This AOL has stolen countless hours of my life just as I am sure the internet has done to the majority of you who are reading these words. I mention in the pages ahead about this but I need to share one last story with you the reader, not that you care or anything about what I have to say. I am just a nobody, No Fame No wealth. No Wife No Life, P.S. Only kidding kinda on that last comment there, but you get my point. I am not Brad Pitt so let's just get that straight. And because I am a nobody, my options are limited. No excuses here, just the truth. Because of the internet everybody's options at normal social interaction has become limited. This personal computer has ruined society whether you wanna believe it or not. Its great for information and quick communication but it pulls you in like a drug. Addicting to say the least. Just the way America On Line Likes it. More money for them, and every other internet company. I'm not knocking it completely but please. It has gotten out of control. It's not real folks'. Don't you get it??? That's why we spend so much time on this freaking thing called a computer. It leaves an emptiness in our heart, mind, soul and

Physical being. By this I mean, P.S. Now pay attention here this is very important. "Our natural needs are not being met by interacting with another human being in person". That is why we keep signing on. Something in us wants more but we never get it from a computer monitor. One big Lie from the Devil to keep you coming back for more. He knows if he can keep you distracted that you won't be doing what God wants each and everyone of us to be doing. And that is to be sharing our Lives with each other in a loving way. A little bit of the computer is not a bad thing but I think most people are way out of balance with this technology stuff. It is not reality folk's, wake up. Just like the commercials on Stupid Bowl Sunday. Perfect example is this pizza commercial. What they are trying to accomplish with this here false advertisement is, "Ok, get this now, The poor slob with the beer in his hand will think he has got a shot at getting in the sack with this little vixen holding the large pie with meatball's walking right towards his dumb ass while he sits on the couch watching his buddies new, Five foot plasma screen hella vision. Number 1, He ain't got no shot in hell at having sex with Jessica Simpson. Number 2, After he eats that large pie with meat ball's the only thing he is getting is ogada and a-"upset stomach" and a bad case of soon to come constipation. Poor bastard, he has no clue about the truth just like I didn't 10 years ago either.

Hey, you know what, It sounds like to me that I am a little jealous and bitter that she ain't coming over to my house after the game either. Besides, I still live with my Mom so she probably would have a problem with that like most high falutin females this day and age. Did I spell "faluten" right???? If you don't know what falutin means come to Wrong Island New York and go into a local store or mall and you will find the definition right there. Boy , I am a little bitter, ain't I? Just realistic in my opinion. No one cares about my opinion any way. Alllll righty then, where was I? Oh yes The Stupid Bowl, Godadddy .com or some shit had to keep submitting there commercial because they wanted to see how low they can go. How sexist is to much sexist. Hey, maybe Janet Jackson can show both boobs this year. Wardrobe malfunction again. One big Lie my friends, just one big Lie. Stop falling for it America. Boycott these worthless games and spend more time with your family and friends. I promise you it will be more rewarding if you did.

Back to the poor drunken slob who goes home after the Super, oops, I mean Stupid Bowl, all horned out from the commercials and Lingerie bowl. Yet now he has a big problem on his hands. His wife is a Jenny Craig candidate, like me, and she just don't cut the mustard for him like she once did in their younger years. Oh well, time for a divorce I guess. The grass is not greener on the other side buddy. You will still have to mow it, I assure you. While I am at it, The Jerry Springer and Maury Povich show. Do people really watch this???????? Has this country hit rock bottom or what? Like its a big joke. Amazing, absolutely amazing. More like very pathetic and sad if you ask me. Then again, who asked me?. Certainly not President Bush, that's for sure. I think we need Hillary Clinton in Office. She will definitely save America. Yeah right. She could get advice from Bill on how to keep your pants on while in office. I could just see it now. Her first attempt at changing the constitution would probably be, mandatory Gucci pocket books for all females outside of the home. Jesus Christ will role over in Heaven if she is elected. Then again, how much worse can she be then these other fellas out there? Scary thought, that's for sure. We need Arnold Shorts are Bigger, I mean Schwarzeneggar, As our President. P.S. Did I spell Schwarznegerar right? Who cares, Where's my Hummer and Cell phone, I need to get out of this nightmare. I think I'll head to Canada before this book gets published because I am certain I will be evicted from Wrong Island New York for telling the truth about what's going on in this country. I can see it now. Big Arnold, on the steps of the white house with Vise President Louis Devito by his side. Ordering mandatory Testosterone shots once a week for all men 13 years of age and older. At least he can make me laugh a little bit here and there. President Bush bores the hell out of me. Wouldn't it be great if all men where on steroids in America. We think we got problems now, holy mackeral. I think we should give it a shot. Just like all the baseball players give each other a shot in the ass of testosterone so they can hit more home runs and make more money. I mean that's what it's all about right? MONEY. I don't think so pal, so wake up and stop thinking only about yourself Mister Businessman. Start helping out the little people once in a while. Wishful thinking on my part. This country is demon possessed. Oh Boy, That comment will definitely get me sent to Iraq.

That's why at exactly 7:27 PM on Stupid Bowl Sunday I am writing these words instead of wasting my time letting America influence me on the hella vision. The Devil ain't getting me no more if I can help it. I sure am a party pooper ain't I?? I love sports, so don't get me wrong. It is the messy business side that turns me off these day's. Give Roger Maris back his home run record will ya. Ahhhhh yes, We have reached all new lows, then again I still think there might be some room left after this pathetic attempt at entertainment. Get A load of this. You may even be watching it right now as I type these words. "The Lingerie Bowl". Amy Fisher and Joey Butafucko finally reunited after she shot his wife in the head. Both Morons starting on each others respective goal line walking towards one another to the 50 yard line where I think his ex wife Mary Jo will flip the coin to see which group of broads, "with hardly any clothes on". Will receive the Kick off. I could be wrong on some of the particulars of this new game called the Lingerie Bowl because I have yet to see it played. What kind of Low Life losers produce a show like this??? Shot your Lovers wife in the head and become an overnight star. Only in America". Do you think they are getting paid for this coin toss????? Daaaaaaa, maybe! Can't get any lower than this. Come back Lord Jesus, Please come back soon, I can't take it anymore

Now for my last stupid story. Because I don't do the bar thing and I live on Wrong Island, I mean Long Island New York, meeting people is very difficult. Everyone so caught up with them selves. Very little sincerity left out there. Enter AOL Christian Chat room. I never spoke with so many liers in my Life. Did I spell Liers right????? Any one, any one, Whatever, who cares. These females claiming to be Christians and telling me that they booked a flight to come visit my dumb ass and even giving me flight numbers and all. One problem though, There where no flights coming from there home town to Lagaurdia airport that day. Amazing! I'm sure most of you reading about this could give to craps about my non existent social life, yet I hope you see what I am trying to get at. "What The Hell is going on out there in this country America, can somebody please tell me???

"America On Lies"

Boy ain't this the truth, from the government on down. That is where it all starts folks, our ungodly government. These people running our nation need to take a long hard look back into history and educate themselves on the founders and forefathers of America. Speaking of education, that is the only reason a good majority of our politicians are in office. They are sure not there because of their knowledge of Bible based principles, that's for sure. This goes for the, Mega corporations, Mr. businessman, Educational institutions, Family households, even churches I am sad to say and the list goes on. "In God We Trust", go ahead, look at all those dollars and coins you got in your pocket. What it say on them? Hmmmmmm. Maybe that's a misprint, counterfeit, that's what is. Afraid not Pal. There is a real big important reason why it says that on all your big bucks Buddy, which by the way, will one day be worth nothing soon. You see my friend, where there is no God, there is no good. That's why this country is in such a mess. This country is in a downward spiral as you watch these politicians try to take God out of everything. There is no more shame or morals in this country. It's disgusting. I'm 40 years old and it is mind-boggling to me how far we have fallen in just the last 10 years. We think the Internet and all this technology is progress. Well let me tell you. It's one big lie. It's slowly wiping out the world.

I'm no scholar as you will soon find out, but I'm no fool either. If you don't program yourself, then the world will program you. That's exactly what's happening to you my dear friends. It's all about money, bottom line. "The Dangers of The Last Days", Here's a little warning for you all. It's in the second book of Timothy. Oh, I forgot to tell you what, "Book". The name of the book is called, P.S. You're not going to like this, I assure you. Has nothing to do with Harry Potter or any other fantasy story. This is the real deal, whether you like or not. OK ready, put your seat belt on and hold on to your hat. You'll probably close this book up real fast, once I tell you. Oh, what the heck, your loss if you do pal. The name of the book is called the Bible.

OK, see you later, have fun in fantasy land on the computer and playing with your cellphone. Wow, what a clear picture on that new five-foot plasma screen TV you got there. Now you can see the devil even clearer. One big lie my friends. Just one big lie. I think I'll open up the Bible and read that second book of Timothy while you guys get nowhere fast. I will read it too you, OK. Now I know I'm asking for a lot but, turn your cell phone off and shut the computer down. If the televisions on, hit the off button on your remote. Now pay attention, It goes like this.

" The Dangers of The Last Days"

You should also know this, Timothy, that in the last days there will be very difficult times. For people will love only themselves and their money. They will be boastful and proud, scoffing at God, disobedient to their parents, and ungrateful. They will consider nothing sacred. They will be unloving and unforgiving; they will slander others and have no self control; They will be cruel and have no interest in what is good. They will betray their friends, be reckless, be puffed up with pride, and love pleasure rather than God. They will act as if they are religious, but they will reject the power that could make them godly. You must stay away from people like that.

Wow, how bout them there words, ha? It's like reading the front and back page of every newspaper in this country. Can someone please tell me how a major-league baseball player wants to be paid $84 million for seven years of service? But we dumb Americans keep buying into this crap and refuse to wake up and smell the coffee. Here yee, Here yee, from me the jerk, to you the moron. Stop going to these professional sporting events for one whole year. Do I have to say it again? I thought so, now listen up. Stop going to these professional sporting events for one whole year. Than watch how fast these cry baby greedy owners and players come back down to earth and join the rest of us working slobs. What a pair of Base"balls" these characters got, let me tell you. $84 million dollars, What the hell does this moron need $84 million dollars for? I have never once seen or heard a professional ball player of any sport say how sorry he feels for the fan that has to pay all that money for a seat and a hot dog to watch his spoiled ass. Never have I heard an owner of these Professional, P.S. I use the word professional, lightly here, sports teams talk about how tough it must be for a fan to attend these waste of time "Game's". Did you get that last word? I said, "Game's" That's all it is, a "Game". What a joke. While I am at it, how about the homerun record that was broken with all these guys taken steroids. And then when they went to court each and every one of them lying about using steroids. One guy told the truth, so he can write a book and make money. He thinks that steroids should be legal and people in sports should be allowed to take them. I think he mentioned how at one time in his career he was the best baseball player on the planet. Yet he didn't mention that thanks to all the steroids he was pumping into him was the only reason he was on the ball field in the first place. These guys make me laugh. What makes me laugh even harder is the American public buying into this crap. It's actually not funny at all, kinda makes me sad. Give back the home-run record to Roger Maris, who it belongs to. Didn't I say that already??? One big lie my friends, just one big lie. Bottom line folks is, that it's all our fault. We buy into it.

Human beings would not miss any of these sports if they were not played. It's just a big lie, us hoping that our team beats the other team. Who the heck cares. Look in the mirror folks and concentrate on your family, friends, wife and or husband if you got one and most importantly, your poor children who are exposed to all this garbage. One big deception on were their happiness will be coming from. This country has got us all duped, faked out I am telling you right now, something has got to be done folks.

America is not going to last much longer without God in our governments, corporations, schools and most importantly, households. It all starts in the family household. If Mommy and Daddy are not teaching the word of God and the fundamental teachings of Jesus Christ to their children then what do we expect? Bottom line, "No God", "No Good". And I hope I just offended you with that comment if you're not a believer, "Yet", the truth is an offense to those who don't want to hear it, period. There was once a time when I was a know it all. Bottom line was, I didn't know anything. Had to teach and learn for myself, the hard way. The best way, I must admit. So I know how you feel right now after reading these last few sentences and or paragraphs. I would be just about ready to close this here stupid book up, head to the fridge, grab myself a cold brewski, and sit down on that nice lazy boy sofa I got there in my living room and turn that television, "hella" vision on, so I could get fed some more lies from the media and corporations advertising what they want me to think will make me happy if I go buy their product. Oh, and while I am at it, let me check my cell phone to see if anyone has called in the last four in half seconds. These cell phones are like the plague. This godforsaken gadget has got a major grip on society. The lovely state of New York has a law against these evil nemesis to society yet every 6 out of 10 people driving a vehicle has these mind numbing gadgets welded to their stupid selfish heads. No regard for the law or their fellow man. Even cops driving their patrol cars and firemen in the chief trucks using these freaking things while they are driving. Excellent example gentleman, excellent example, if I do say so myself. Nobody gives a hoot anymore. Anything goes, no morals or values left. Once again, No God, No good. I heard the other day how when there are no Bible based principles in a nation or society, the result is chaos. Noooooooo, Really? This country is a mess, starting from the top of the government and leader in charge. Cough, Cough, excuse me, I just had a clear my throat. Leader in charge. Scary thought, I must admit, anyway, right on down to the eight year-old waiting at the bus stop to go to school with his pants hanging down past his ankles, basketball jersey 22 sizes to big for him and his baseball cap on backwards. P.S. Does this little lost soul actually think he looks good???? The battery in his television "Hella" vision remote control must have died and the channel on his TV must be stuck on MTV. What a sight these kids. Speaking of kids, why is the 13 year-old girl standing next to him waiting to go to school look like a future stripper wearing jeans four sizes too small for her and a shirt that has her whole stomach and breast's sticking out??????? Anyone, Anyone, Bueller, Bueller.

You know, maybe I'm just becoming an old fart my old age. I don't know. Thank God if I am. I must admit when I was that age I was lost as well. I did not come from a Bible based home. Neither did my mom and dad. It's all passed down from generation to generation my friends. Someone has to break the curse. If I can wake a few people up before God calls me home, then all the better. Well, I hope God calls me home. The first 30 years of my life was out of control. I have repented for my sins though folks and continue to do so every day. We're all sinners and God knows this. That is why he sent his son Jesus into the world to atone for our sinful nature so that one day we could be caught up with God in heaven for eternity. But, Noooooo, not us Americans, we deserve the best down here in the world. Can you imagine how God is looking at this country right now??? I give my children everything and then some of their hearts desire. And the overwhelming majority of these people give me nothing, no time, no thanks, just more, more, more, is all they want.

Real quick, you know what would be really cool? When Jesus comes back to earth, I wonder if he will have a cell phone. Wouldn't it be great if all these jerks and idiots driving their car breaking the law with these God forsaken gadgets welded to their head and the people walking in a daze out in public with these freaking things attached to the side of their no brain head, P.S. Was this a run on sentence? I think it was. Anyway, it would be great if all of a sudden, everybodie's cellphone got interrupted in the middle of their meaningless conversations and Jesus was on the other side of the line. I bet he would say, I interrupt this "broadcast"-"Phone call" to bring you a special bulletin. This is Jesus Christ calling and my question to you is, " Why have you never called on me all these years in your life"???

I give you 24 hours a day, seven days a week and you never even called me once to say thank you for your life and luxuries I have given you. I'm very angry at all of you. Now put your cell phone's down, stop your car, and get out of it. Walk to the side of the road, so I don't run you over, and get on your hands and knees and pray as if your life depended on it, because it does my sons and daughters, let me tell you, it does. And just maybe, just maybe, if I'm in a good mood, I might save your soul from hell for not honoring me down here on earth, Amen. Now stay down there on your knees until I give you permission to get up. You people need a hard dose of humility to get rid of all that selfishness and pride. In the meantime, I think I will go buy myself a computer and sign on to "America on Lies" and let the world know through one big instant message and e-mail, "That I am back, and it's no Lie". "Judgment Time Has Come". You sit in front of your computer for hours at a time. You sit in front of your television for hours at a time. You shop until you drop. You eat until your belly is full. Satisfy all your fleshly desires, P.S. which is never satisfied, drive around in luxury vehicles, participate and or watch every activity under the sun, I give you all of this, all of this I give you, I say again, "And you give me Nothing". No thanks, no acknowledgment, nothing, like I never existed. You think because you can't see me, that I can't see you. Oh so wrong America, Oh so wrong. I give you a government with a set of rules and laws that were founded on my father God's principles. Yet you foolish people are about to die in the devil's dirty ways. Why, why, I ask you? "In God We Trust" it says it right there on all the loot and cash you carry around in your pocket to remind you, who gave this all to you. Now you're trying to take me out of your government, schools, corporations and households. Oh my I say, Oh my. This is not good, my wayward sons, this is not good. How many signs and wonders do you need in order for you to repent and ask me for forgiveness? Tell me, how many more? You have all the wealth in the world, materialisticly speaking. Yet you live one big lie, because you really are, very poor. Very, Very, Poor. Quick proverb for you Americans. "Rich people picture themselves as wise, but their real poverty is evident to the poor." OK then,

I'm using my faithful, yet still a little on the jerky boy side, servant here, Mark, to warn you about what's gonna happen if you don't repent and acknowledge me for all your good gifts that come from my father God above. He is just a no body, this Mark I choose. Here's a quick quote from my book that I wrote, "The Bible". Remember, dear brothers and sisters, that few of you were wise in the world's eyes, or powerful, or wealthy when God called you. Instead, God deliberately chose things the world considers foolish in order to shame those who think they are wise. And he chose those who are powerless to shame those who are powerful. God chose things despised by the world, things counted as nothing at all, and used them to bring to nothing what the world considers important, so that no one can ever boast in the presence of God. All right, then.

My servant Mark was once lost like most of you, yet he at least keeps coming back to me even when he screws up, which I'm must admit, he does often. Yet I like and love his persistence and tenacity. No longer a quitter like he was in high school. He was drinking alcohol and smoking that funny weed stuff, which really is a big lie. He didn't know any better, so I forgave and forgive him. So I now ask you America?

Hey, don't you move, keep your head down and remain on your knees. I'm not even close to being done here with you. Now my question is, this here Mark fella, I have put a thorn in his side, he is constantly in pain. I give him no wife, very little money, no friends, the poor bastard, "P.S. ooops, sorry, just telling the truth," has messed up for three-quarters of his life so far and has to live in the same room he lived in as a child because all that weed he smoked stole his motivation. I have even let Satan attack him for the last 10 years straight, and yet still, I say again, and yet still, he thanks me every day and never gets mad at me. He knows I need a fellow like him who is willing to suffer for the kingdom of God my father in order for him to spread the good news that, I and my father are the only way to eternal life.

But, Noooo, I say, Noooooo, not you fat cats that I give everything to. Never even give me a passing thought unless in a fit of anger or rage you will call my name out, "Jesus Christ". Well I hate to tell you, I can't hear you. Must be a bad connection on that there cell phone I want you to throw into the fire. I tell you now, It is better that your cell phone end up in the fire, rather than your soul. But it's okay, keep going on your merry way thinking all is well. I tried warning you that this day would come. But you never opened the book I gave you all, "The Bible", and searched for the scripture. "I will come as a thief in the night, when you least expect it". Wellll, surprise. I'm back, and I got lots of work to catch up on. Excuse me, Mark, yes Jesus, take a break for bit my faithful son. You look exhausted.

Sit down next to me, I'll takeover from here, thank you Jesus. These people are wearing me out Lord. I am tired, you're right Lord. Thank-you for noticing. Relax my son, take a nap. I'll wake you up when I'm done with these characters. OK, then. I'm not as mad as you think. Because you have all been lied to. All this technology crap is from my next-door neighbor, "the devil". You actually think it is making life easier and better but your lives have gotten harder and worse. You have been deceived. But I'm here to give you the truth, and the truth shall set you free.

You know what? I'm actually still very mad at you all because I have given you a conscience and a will. The knowledge of me is intuitively hard wired into each and every one of you. Here's a word you'll understand. I "Downloaded", myself into every one of you from the day you were born. So you have no excuse for not being my friend and calling on me from day to day. I'm the best friend you would and could ever have. Yet you abandoned me and leave me out of your life. So with that being said, I think I will get a good night's sleep while each and every one of you tremble with fear as you remain on your hands and knees. And just maybe, just maybe, when I get up tomorrow, I will show some mercy on you all and let you stand back up so you could look up in the sky that I created and start begging me for forgiveness. But until I tell you, stay down there on your knees where you should have been every once in awhile all these years. I tried warning each and every one of you, but you did not listen. "Now I am back". Goodnight, and see you tomorrow. P.S. Mark, yes Jesus, get off your knees and go try and get some sleep. You look terrible buddy. Yet I'm very proud of you my son, a job well done. See you in the morning my son, Good night Jesus, thank you for everything. Welcome Mark, sweet dreams pal, Amen.

Morning Mark, Morning Jesus. So I here this, AMERICAONLIES. com, P.S. Actually small letters, I was just trying to make a point to you the reader, with the capital leters. americaonlies.com, is actually owned by America Online, you say? Yes Sir Jesus, Hmmmmmm, very interesting. So my children are being deceived ha? Sure looks that way to me Jesus. One big lie, they sit in front of a monitor and think it's reality when its not reality at all Just one Corporation, claiming to be America, what Mark? America Online, Lord? The majority of the population is hooked on this Internet stuff Lord. The people of America are like Internet junkies. I must admit Jesus that it pulls you in, puts you like in a trance. Yes I know Mark, just the way my neighbor the devil like's it. Please don't get me wrong Lord, It's great for information and communication long distance. Even for business it comes in handy as well. But other than that Lord, this Internet has ruined society in my opinion. Yes I know, I know Mark. All this had to happen, before I came back. P.S. Real quick Jesus, I just want to thank you for coming back to earth. I was getting very lonely, no one likes me because of my allegiance to you. Well not no one, there are few believers I come across here and there. But not many Jesus, not many. I know Mark, I know Mark. Don't worry pal, I got it all under control now. Everything is under "My Control" now. Hey Mark, yes Jesus. So what do you think I should do with all these people. Should I show them mercy, or hand them over to my next door neighbor for the frying pan? Oh please Lord, please, that is not for me to answer Lord. That question is the biggest question ever for mankind Lord. Well come on pal, help me out here. You seem to have worked through most of your anger management problems. I'm still very pissed off at all these people, even after a good night's sleep. Oh and by the way, how did you sleep last night Mark, my son? Not good again Lord Jesus, not good at all. You see Lord I was totally broke and cracked a joke about living under the Brooklyn Bridge in that last book I wrote and now I had no choice but to take a job driving an auto parts truck and guess where they send me every day Lord? I don't have to guess Mark, I already know. You drive under the Brooklyn Bridge every day for 11 bucks an hour on the books. Well you asked for it Mark, so I gave it to you. You gave it to me all right Jesus. That's for sure. C'mon Mark, lighten up, where is your sense of humor? Remember? That thorn in your side. I have to keep you humble. Otherwise you might end up like the rest of these characters I am about to deal with. You're right Jesus, you're right.

I do appreciate the job you gave me Lord. Because 11 bucks an hour is better than nothing, that's for sure. I got a ticket yesterday Jesus, for parking in front of a fire hydrant. $115.00 bucks, that's two days pay. Now I can't buy my turkey sandwich for lunch. Don't worry Mark, what I feed you is eternal, lasts forever. Besides, you need to drop a couple pounds any way my son. You're right Lord, you're always right.

Alllll righty then Marky boy, were should I start next? The government, Hollywood, corporations, Mr. businessman, World wide Web, family households, woman dressed in suggestive clothing, talk to me Mark, Flip a coin with my father's name on it. Please Jesus, don't ask me these questions. Only you could decide and judge mankind and the world. Okay Mark, you're right. Take a seat next to me again, you still look shot again today. You can say that again Lord. OK then Mark, how ironic that your Bible is opened to the last book of Proverbs on your hamper in the bathroom Why don't you write down what it says in the last paragraph there, OK Jesus, here it goes.

Charm is deceptive, and beauty does not last. But a woman who fears the Lord will be greatly praised. Reward her for all she has done. Enough said, OK then, let's start with all the women and young adults walking around with suggestive clothing. Listen up ladies, or shall I say, "Cover-Up". Why do you feel the need to bare as much as possible? Are you starving for attention that bad? The only attention you should be looking for is from me. I took a rib out of my faithful son Adam, "And Made You". Then I told you not to eat from one tree, and yet you did not listen. I gave you everything, yet you wanted more. Obviously things have not changed one bit since back then on that day. You're still never satisfied. I understand though, Your mom and dad are not doing their job at home. Mommy and Daddy have to work so hard to keep that huge house afloat and those big shiny fancy metal things you use to get around in. Boy oh boy, back in my day, I had to walk around everywhere I needed to go, with holes in my moccasins. Man, have things changed. Speaking of man, I feel sorry for you guys with the way all these women are presenting themselves. It's only natural for you fellas to look at a beautiful looking woman. That's why I said to cover-up ladies. Proverbs: A woman should show her beauty by her inner character, not her suggestive clothing. C'mon ladies, you could look just as attractive in contemporary conservative clothing. Why let it all hang out for all to see? Well, I am waiting for an answer? Just what I thought, you got no answer. Because it's all you see on TV and newspapers and in stores. All right, I guess I can forgive you on this one for the time being. But here is my command: Cover-up, get your nose's out of the sky, lose all that American arrogant pride you have developed over the last 10 to 20 years and start reading the word of God, "The Bible". Stop thinking your better then men and for heaven's sakes, please, I say please, do not watch any more of these Desperate housewives episodes. This stuff is poison for your soul and a terrible influence on your wardrobe. Now go and sin no more. Your sins are forgiven, Amen.

Okay Mark, wake up sleepyhead. My first job is done. Where should I start next? Who's next on my list? I'm not even worthy to have a conversation with you or be in your presence. So would you please stop asking me for advice. But if you don't mind I would like to ask you a question Lord. Shoot Mark, I'm ready. Can you believe they're finally getting around to investigating what happened to all the money that was donated to the 9-11 fund, four years after the fact? Only problem is, "They", meaning the people who are doing the investigating, are probably just as corrupt as the people who were in charge of the 9-11 funds. I did hear that the mayor was kind enough to give his new girlfriend, P.S. not his wife, a good paying job during all this. I could be wrong though. Why didn't he give me a job Jesus? Well Mark, probably because you neglected to go to college and you're not his girlfriend. Oh, OK, thanks Jesus, I was just curious. Hmmmmmmm, sounds like to me you want me to start my judgment with the government now Mark? Sure, what the heck Jesus, go for it. I hope you ate your Wheaties this morning Lord, because you've got your hands full on this one. Just take a seat Mark, you still look a little beat up today from all this evil you are surrounded by. Just be thankful I saved you from all this chaos. Which I know you are. That's why I am letting you sit next to me my son. I am proud of you. That your living in this world, but you are no longer of the world. This sort of talk confuses the nonbelievers of my father in heaven. But don't you worry Markey Boy, By the time I'm done down here, everyone will be a believer whether they like it or not. Praise my father God, Amen.

Here yee, here yee. For all you politically correct hot shots and greedy nonbelievers of my father God. I order all of you out from behind your fat desks. Wait a second, Mark, wake up. You told me I could take a nap Lord. I said take a seat, not a nap. Anyway, I need a hand again here, I don't know what to do with all these characters. I came back to save sinners from eternal damnation, but for crying out loud these guys just don't listen. How many warnings do they need before they open back up the history books and see how this country was founded. "On my father God's principles. Not their own self-serving agendas. Man oh man Mark, this one has got me concerned and confused. What a ya say we have them join all the cellphone abuses still on their hands and knees on the side of the road trembling with fear? Because let me tell you something sleepyhead, I mean Mark my son. If there is anyone I would like to run over with my Hummer, it would be all of these clowns. My father tells me to forgive them, for they know not what they do. Not so fast though, I need some sincere repentance from these fat cats. This may take some time.

Now listen up all you corrupt tax collectors and leaders of the country that I gave you all. And pay attention good, I burn with anger that you want to take "Christ" out of Christmas. I now hear you also want to take "In God We Trust" off your currency that you don't even thank me for. Have any of you ever met my neighbor? Of course you have, he is your cousin and you know him well. I will tell each and every one of you that you're all bad judge of character when it comes to your close relative. I forgive you all because he is the great deceiver and King of all Lies. My good old next door neighbor, "The devil", Satan himself.

No excuse, Now stand up straight and look me in the eye. Hmmmmmm, just what thought. You can't look me in the eye, I think I mentioned that before. Hey, nobody's perfect. You're perfect Jesus, Shush Mark, you know that, but I don't want them to know or they will never accept me, even when I'm standing right in front of them. They need to know or think that I am like them, or my father God and I will never soften their hearts so they can turn to us and let him and I heal them. The sad part is that, 99 percent of them don't even think they are wounded. Boy oh boy, my next-door neighbor's good at deceiving "All My Children", isn't he Mark? Yes Sir Lord, Yes Sir.

You know something Mark, every human being alive has no excuse for not acknowledging my father in heaven on a daily basis. Look what my father has given them all. I know this might not make sense to the people who are starving to death and or sick with an illness, yet most of them people acknowledge my father even more. It's backwards, ha Mark. Yes Jesus, very much so.

12-22-05. How many times do I have to tell you to stay off of America On Lies Mark? Ha, How many? How did you know, I was on there. Don't play smart with me Mark, I know everything, so don't even go there Mr. funnyman. I know Jesus, but this loneliness is killing me. And I feel even more lonely after I go on the computer. It's one big lie Lord, there really is no one even there. You talk with people who you don't even know what they really look like or how they truly feel. They can type anything they want you to believe, No eye contact though Lord. Well then, why do you keep going back for more? I believe it is Satan, Lord, working on my weaknesses. There you go Mark, now your getting it. Now stop listening to Satan and finish writing this here book so America can find out what deception my neighbor has in store for all of them next. What deception Lord, I mean c'mon, how much worse can it get Jesus. Ohhhhhhh, you will see Mark, you will see. This is nothing compared to what the people of this country will one day witness. They will all tremble with fear, the ones who don't know me and my father. Oh Boy Jesus, Boy oh boy, not good for them ha? I'm afraid not Mark, I'm sorry son.

Jesus, I know we're jumping around here on topics and subject matter but, I had a terrible day driving all over Brooklyn and Queens today. Traffic everywhere due to the New York City transit strike. I think they want more money. I'm sure this does not surprise you Lord. Nope, sure don't Mark, any way Lord. Do you mind if I take a break tonight, I wanna read your book "The Bible" instead. I need some strength so I am gonna feed on you and your father's word for a bit. Go ahead Mark, that's why I wrote that book. Yet not many realize this, I'm afraid not many at all my son. The majority of women feel it is man written. This bothers them to begin with. Yet they never even opened it up and they judge it and condemn it. What they don't know is I was the one who inspired men to write it. Their minds are closed and their hearts are hardened Mark. My neighbor has done a good job on all of them. Anyway Mark, take your time and build your strength back up. And besides, this will give me more time to figure out how I'm going to proceed with the people of America. When you feel better and stronger c'mon back and we will continue with the government like I said I would. Ok Lord, sounds good. Good night Jesus, sweet dreams, you to Mark, you to my son.

Ok Mark, wake up sleepyhead, you sure sleep alot. I don't have much time Mark and I need to finish up down here. What would you like me to do with the government. Please don't ask me for advice Lord, I'm not even worthy of your presence. Lighten up partner, this is why the majority don't hang out with me. They think I am boring and no fun to be around. Just more lies that my next-door neighbor keeps filling their heads with. Wait a second Mark, you don't listen either do you? How many times do I have to tell you to stay off of America On Lies? You're not going to find your future wife in a Christian chat room, I assure you for crying aloud. Man your stubborn, the devil loves pulling you in there. I give him permission all the time. But all you have to do is keep your eyes on me and the future and you won't fall for his tricks and lies, Ok Buddy? Yes Jesus. Please forgive me once again. It's just that I get lonely sometimes, why don't you give me mate Lord? That is for me to know and you to find out Mark. Now just keep doing what I say and don't question me. In my time, Mark, remember? In my time, not yours. You don't play fair Jesus. Hey, watch the lip, have I ever let you down before? No Lord, I'm sorry. Okay then, keep writing, yes sir. Real quick Jesus, if I keep making believe I'm having this conversation with you in this book everyone is going to think I'm nuts. What are you talking about Mark, everyone already thinks you're nuts. The majority of the people just don't get. Be glad my son, for a great reward awaits you in heaven, Amen. Okey-doke Lord, I hear ya, thank you very much, praise God, Amen.

Dear Lord. Yes Mark? I have to share this with you real quick, if you don't mind. Sure, what is it Mark? Someone close to me just told me that the people close to her, "Know" God, in their own way. I immediately responded, there's no such thing. I am on to something here Jesus, hear me out. There's only "One Way" to knowing God I responded, not our own way. There is the problem right there Lord, "Own Way". People only want to know God your father on their own terms, their own way. Major, major, lie, from your neighbor, Jesus. You can say that again Mark. "Own Way, Own way, Wow Jesus. Humans want to do it their own way and here's where the major problem lies Lord. Very true mark very true my son, excellent observation, excellent. OK then Mark, with that being said, any other questions for me, because I'm going to be very busy for the next couple of hours and days ahead. Lots of work for me to do here. Oh sorry Lord, this may take a bit, but I want to share one more story with you. OK then, stand up Mark and let me sit down for this one, I am going to need the rest for the days ahead. My pleasure Jesus, please sit, please. All right Mark, talk to me, what happened today that you feel such urgency to share with me. Take your time Mark, you and I got forever pal, maybe not so for all these people on their hands and knees.

Begin, OK Lord. Please save this country and its people Lord. It needs alot of help. No kidding Mark, that's why I'm here talking with you. Get out there and warn everyone, I am trying Lord. I know Mark. Just busting your chops a little bit. I am proud of you my son, and you know it. Yes I do Lord and I am grateful for your praise, Amen. Tell me Mark what happened today while you were driving around Brooklyn and Queens.

Well Lord, I had never been to Coney Island before, by the amusement park, beach and boardwalk and on my last delivery I was only two blocks away so I went to see it and take a walk along the boardwalk and stroll down to the ocean. I saw the original famous Nathan's Hot dog place were Bugsy Siegel used to go for his hot dogs before he came up with the idea in Las Vegas, "Sin" city. You know Jesus, where all the gambling is. Anyway, I just want to write down exactly what I did when I was sitting in the van looking at the cyclone roller-coaster. 12-21-05. I am at Coney Island right now Lord Jesus. I'm gonna take a walk on the beach and boardwalk and thank you for giving me another day in this world and Country America. Here is the strange part lord. This guy named Roman, who owns the body Shop, pays cash for his parts and just the other day he gave me a $10 tip. I couldn't believe it. I thought I was rich. Took me all day to try and figure out what to do with that 10 bucks. So you're that broke, ha Mark? Financially speaking, yes Jesus. But I am rich with the Holy Spirit. Thanks to you and your father God. That's the spirit Markey Boy, good answer my son. Now please continue, I am starting to like some of your crazy stories if you can believe that. Only kidding Mark, proceed, yes Lord.

Ok then, it was freezing for a December Day, four days before your birthday. As I walked up the ramp, oh wait a second, I forgot to mention, remember the nice generous gentleman woman who gave me the 10 bucks the other day? Yes I do Mark, how could I forget him. All right then lord. The guy just gave me another tip for $7 dollars. I said thank-you so much sir, no one else does this. I think he saw in my eyes how much I not only needed the seven bucks but even more importantly so, how much I appreciated it. OK then, me and my seven bucks start walking to the top of the pier and I see a man sipping soup out of a container sitting on the bench. I nodded and said hello, but he did not acknowledge me. Anyway, I couldn't believe it, here I was, at the famous Coney Island boardwalk. I walked past the bathrooms on to the sand and strolled down to the ocean. When I got to the surf, I spoke with you, as you recall. Thanked you for my life, then turned around and soaked in the Coney Island amusement park, which I never seen before. As I was freezing my buns off, I started heading back to the boardwalk. Oh, real quick Lord. Did you hear my prayer about asking you to bring me a real true faithful, loyal Christian wife? P.S. I know this is a major request Lord in these crazy days, but I have faith in you. I know you can pull one out of the hat for your good buddy Mark. What did I tell you Mark? I said in my time, not yours. But keep on asking and you shall receive. Real funny Jesus, you got that one out of the Bible. No kidding Mark, that's because I wrote it. Now keep telling your story. You got five more minutes because I have got to get to work, if you know what I mean. I thought you said we had all the time in the world Jesus? We do Mark, Just playing with you a bit, relax pal.

OK Lord, as I am walking back toward the boardwalk, I passed the bathrooms and I look to the left and I see a few people freezing like me as they stroll along the boardwalk. I then look to my right and see a few more brave souls. I keep walking toward the van and sure enough, I see the man still sipping his probably cold soup by now. I think he was a homeless man Jesus. Yes he was Mark, now continue. Well anyway Lord, I felt terrible. The pastor at the church I attend once in awhile said Sunday that we should not feel bad or guilty for not giving these people help if possible. I so disagree Jesus, I so disagree. I don't think this pastor has ever seen a hard day like this poor guy Lord. Not judging him, but c'mon. Now I know what I'm about to say next might turn people away from you even more Lord. Not that it takes people much to not acknowledge you, anyway. The preacher starts saying how his online appliance business is doing great and he just took a $36,000 order. That's a little tough for a guy like myself to hear, especially when I asked him if he needed any help even just one day a week and he never gave me a job. Well anyway Jesus, as I reached into my pocket while walking toward the poor man drinking his cold soup freezing his butt off, I give him a couple dollars for a cup of coffee. I say here, go get a cup of coffee. He thanks me several times. I then noticed on the next bench, another poor soul, lying there sound asleep, snoring like a baby. I was horrified Jesus, this could be me or anyone else. Only your father knows why someone ends up like this. Not the preacher who just shared his new found $36,000 grand off his web site with the few people in the small church. He's a good guy Lord, spreading your father's words, but give me a break. The guys messages have lost their effectiveness ever since he and his wife and kids moved into that House on the water.

These two poor bastards live on the water as well Jesus, but they ain't got no house. Anyway, I try waking him up but he kept snoring. I asked the guy I just gave the other couple bucks to if he could help me wake him up. No use, this guy is snorring like a baby. I was actually jealous of him. I wish I could sleep like that. I asked my new friend again, if he would please give the money I had in my hand to him when he wakes up. He said, no, it's okay. So I try a little harder. As he was snoring away my new friend with the cold soup said he would really appreciate it. I started pushing his shoulder a little harder and shaked him a bit until he came to what ever little senses he had and as he awoke I placed the last of the $7 dollars that Roman gave me into his hand and said go get a cup of coffee. He was so grateful Jesus. Him and his friend kept thanking me over and over again. I then noticed a beer can in a paper bag on top of the picnic table that he was sleeping on and immediately told him, no beer, OK, coffee, no beer. Him and his friend laughed very hard and thanked me over and over again as I slowly walked away, holding back my tears. Terrible Jesus, absolutely terrible. Please help my two new friends Lord, please. Don't worry Mark, those two fellows are coming home to me soon, forever. Thank you Lord, thank you. My question to the pastor is, Do you know how or why these two fellas ended up like this??? Maybe they didn't have a good father or mother as a child. Even yet, maybe they were born and left in a dumpster somewhere in Brooklyn. Who knows, I sure don't. It's not guilt we feel when run home and grab our last 20 bucks and drive back as fast as possible to give the money to these two fellows. It's called compassion, sorrow for another human being and empathy. And yes, maybe a little guilt that Father God gave us much more than these two fellows.

I know you tell us not to tell our right hand what are left hand just did. But I figured I could share this with you because you won't tell anyone Jesus, Amen. I heard on W MCA on 5:70 a.m. Christian radio that when a minister or pastor gives his message on Sunday morning he is really talking to himself as well. So a preacher needs to practice what he preaches. The pastor said we need to find some ministry to support with our money so they can go help others in need. When we help the homeless or poor we are helping God's children, regardless of how or why they got that way. Never judge a man until you walk a mile in his moccasins. OK now Mark, relax. I just want to say thank you for helping my children Mark. When you help the least of mankind, then you are helping me as well. Job well done. Please Lord, it was the least I could do. I don't want any credit for this. It just seemed natural for me to walk over to these two guys. Probably because I can relate to them so good. If it wasn't for my mom I would be sleeping right next to them tonight on the next bench over. Hey Jesus, I just came up with a really cool idea, tell me what you think. Hurry Mark, I'm going to be late for work. OK then, So I think instead of the pastor walking a mile in these guys smelly hole ridden shoes, I got a good idea instead. How about on the night before your birthday Jesus, Christmas Eve, we put my two new friends in the pastors House on the water and him and I can sleep on the two, park bench's on the Coney Island boardwalk near the famous cyclone roller coaster. But before beddy-bye time, we can do a balance transfer. We will put the $36,000 grand the pastor made the other day online with the click of a mouse into my two new friend's pockets. Then the guy sipping the cold soup will transfer his $2 two bucks into my left pocket and the other fella who was sound asleep when I met him, can transfer the five books I gave him into the pastors right pocket. OK then, sound like a plan pastor? I mean what's the big deal Jesus, the pastor still is living on the water right? And so are these two guys. Just in a different neighborhood now. Sweet dreams pastor, and I hope you get a good night's sleep, because I'm looking forward to your message and sermon Christmas morning. Jesus would you come to church with me Christmas morning? And do you think his message would be a little different from last Sunday Jesus? I feel in my heart that it will be a very effective one. I bet the pastor will preach about the story of the Good Samaritan.

Now, Now, Mark. I know your a little upset, but c'mon now. Do you really think we should do this? Yes I do Jesus. Boy, I think I do need to get you a wife. Your out of control Mark. Well I am gonna have to pass on this one and besides, remember? Vengeance is mine saith the Lord, I shall repay those who deserve it. Now relax Mark, will ya. It was a pretty good idea though, where do you come up with these ideas Mark? I'm starting to enjoy your company more and more. Likewise Jesus, likewise. Now go to work on the government and thank you for your time Lord. I will keep my mouth shut for awhile. Please do Mark, now it's my turn. P.S. sorry for chewing your ear off Jesus, is just that I got no one to talk to. Every time I mention you, they run away from me. Mark we will talk later OK? Let me get some work done, OK, sorry Lord.

12-25-05. Happy birthday Jesus, thank you Mark. I just want to look thank-you for coming down over 2000 years ago to save all of us sinners from eternal damnation in hell after we leave this world. It is my pleasure Mark, my pleasure. Unfortunately, as your finding out more and more each day, the majority of the human race has no clue about me and heaven and hell. They are lost Mark, very, very lost I am afraid to say. But you just keep on writing and spreading the good news about my father God and I, because one day soon every knee will bow before my father and give an account for their life here in the world. He's gonna ask why they never called him with them there cell phones of theirs.

The work whistle blows. I have had given you enough time to repent and your time is up. All you had to do was look up into the clear blue sky and across the crystal clear sands that lead to the beautiful oceans waves. Who do you think created all this? Tell me, who? Just what I thought, no answer. Your all scared to death aren't you? Never thought you would have to give an account to me for all your actions down here on earth, did you? Well my neighbor has deceived you and everyone else, yet this is no excuse for you not to read my father's book, The Bible, from time to time. Even just 15 minutes a day with your co-workers, family and friends would and could have made a major difference in your self centered and selfish lives. Now it's my time and it turn. Your fleshly fun is over. Now go get on your hands and knees next to all those cellphone abusers on the side of the road because I just filled up my Hummer at three bucks a gallon of gas and I'm going for a ride now to each and every educational and school institution in this country to clean that mess up as well. You're better off on your hands and knees on the side of the road because I would mow you all down if you're still standing with all that pride of yours. Now get, before I change my mind and pass judgment on you all right now, instead of later. Stay down there until I tell you to get up. Shame on all of you.

Eeeeeeeeeerrrrr, tires squealing as Jesus's Hummer comes to a screaming stop. Door slams, as he enters every school building in this country. Flips the megaphone speaker to the on position, testing, testing, one two three. This is not a test, this is the real thing. This is Jesus Christ and I hear you want to stop saying the pledge of allegiance every morning. Actually, you have stopped. You don't even like to bring me or my father's name up in any of your curriculum's. Hmmmm, this amazes me. If it were not for my father God, you all would not even be alive, teaching all these poor little children of mine, only what you want them to know. Now listen up, without me, you have nothing. You hear me? Mr. schoolteacher so-called educator. It just seems to be the same old story right down from the top to bottom. You take me out of your life and all you got is chaos. When will you finally realize, "No God, No Good". You think you know it all, so I will not waste my time with any of you all either. You will not listen anyway. Now put you chalk and pens down, pick up your briefcases, open them up and let your students take everything you got in them and run it through the paper shredder. That stuff you're teaching these kids ain't working anyway. Look at them, most rebellious generation of kids this country has ever seen. OK, this reminds me, my next stop will be in everybody's family household and living room. It all starts with mom and dad. My next door neighbor has got them all deceived to. Man oh man, hey Mark, yes lord. This is no joke, what a mess America is in. I truly don't know where to start, finish or what. You wanna takeover for me for a minute or two? I need to go to the top of the mountain to regroup. This is gonna take alot out of me. Do you got the keys to your camper upstate, New York, Mark? Oh, you don't want to stay there Lord. I got mice inside of it and its water logged a little bit. The roof sprung a leak a few years back and I can't seem to find the hole. Mark, Mark, Mark, Mark. Did you forget how and where I was born? Out in the cold and in a cave. C'mon now buddy, your camper will be like the penthouse at the Trump Tower for me .I'm a humble guy just like you, so now give me the keys for a couple of days, will ya buddy? I need some R and R. Yes, but Jesus, look, you left all those people with the cell phones and the government hotshots on their hands and knees by the side of the road. Good observation Mark, that's exactly where they will stay until I decide what I am going to do with them. With that being said, listen up Mr. and Mrs. schoolteacher. And I use the word teacher lightly. You see all your close cousins and relatives over there on the curbs of the highways? Go join them immediately and they will tell you what to do. Their all finally getting the hang of it. Drop to your hands and knees and tremble with fear because Jesus is here. Hey Mark, that actually rhymed, pretty funny ha? To think all these people of America never wanted to be my friend, ha? Their loss, I say, their loss. Lost is exactly what they all are, this I say for sure.

Anyway Mark, Do you got any electricity or hot water in that there damp camper I gave you a few years back? No sir, sorry. I did not finish hooking up the electric yet Lord. That's okay Mark, I'll invite my next door neighbor, the devil, upstate, New York as well, for a little R and R. This guy puts off enough heat to keep that whole mountain I gave you five years back, nice and warm. And besides, he likes to tempt me on a regular basis as well. I get a kick out of him.

Thanks for the use of the camper and mountain Mark, I will see when I get back in a couple days. It is my pleasure Jesus, I thank you for lending me the camper and mountain. You're the one who owns everything under the sky Lord. Well, you get my point Mark, thanks buddy. See you when I get back. Yes Lord, I look forward to your return. Enjoy your rest.

All right then Mark, wake up, I am back. Boy oh Boy Lord, you are an early riser. Mind if I just take a shower and put my contacts in? Should take me 15 minutes. You may wanna leave your contacts out Mark, because I don't think you're gonna wanna see what I"m gonna do today. Oh no Lord, is it that bad, has judgment day arrived? Bad news, ha Jesus? Afraid so Mark, I am afraid so. Now take a seat and leave your contacts out, this is gonna be ugly.

Anyway Mark, listen to the conversation I heard while I was upstate in your soggy camper. The American man and American woman on their hands and knees while I pondered what to do with them and this country.

Jesus Christ almighty, I can't believe he came back. Who? Jesus Christ, that's who. I thought that Bible book and God religion stuff was all a big farce. I never even once considered paying any attention to any of that junk. Yeah, me too John. Me too. I had no idea me walking around in suggesting clothing was ungodly and that I should show my beauty by my inner character and not my skimpy clothes. Jesus Christ, I can't believe he's back. Stop cursing and using the Lord's name in vain, Jane, this is no joke. I am terrified for our children, family and friends. Will Jesus judge all them as well? I don't know sweet heart, but from what I can see, there's not one open space from where we are as far as my eyes can see with humans on their hands and knees everywhere, people of all ages. Why, why, I can't believe this, why?

I'll tell you why John and Jane. Each time you said my name in vain, I did not hear and could not listen. Neither of you ever called on me with a sincere heart of repentance. Like I said, all you have to do is wake up in the morning and look up in the sky and the answer would enter your eye. That God my father and I made the sky, so you, would never have to die

Life down here should be preparation for my father's home in heaven Mark, this is a mess my son, what a mess. For all these human beings that I created have no excuse for not acknowledging me with the glory that I deserve. They rather hang with my neighbor Satan and satisfy their flesh instead. Well Mark, that flesh I gave each and every one of them will be gone for 99.9% of each one of them in a hundred years give or take a year or two. Do any of these people own a dictionary with the word, "Eternity", highlighted? Apparently not, no excuse, no excuse whatsoever.

Give me your cell phone Mark. I don't have one Jesus. Oh yeah, I forgot, your like the only person in America On Lies that don't have one of these demonic devices. Didn't I say this already? I am starting to repeat my self like you Mark, must be contagious. All right then, change of plans.

I think I'll open the heavens with a great big bang of thunder and lightning. This should get mom and dad's attention. Baaaaaammmmm! Guess who Mommy and Daddy? Open your front door, it's time to have a talk with your makers Son. Why do you not teach your Sons' and Daughters', the word of God my father? Ha , why? Just what I thought. Because your Mom and Pop didn't teach you either. No Excuse, no excuse at all. No stand up and get out from behind that the demonic computer and television you and your children so much love. You should be sitting at the kitchen table reading the word of God to one another, even if just for a half hour a day. You all can't even give me a half-hour a day, can you? How awful I say, how awful. Look at all I give you, and you give me nothing. No thanks, no praise, no respect, zilch, zippo, ungotz, one big zero is what I get from you. Now listen up and listen up good. I want each one of you knuckleheads to grab your cell phones and on the way out the door on the way to the Hummer limousine I have waiting for you all. I want you to place your cell phones on the ground in front of the great big tires on this godforsaken vehicle. P.S. These great big tires will at least come in handy for something. Now get in the Hummer with the rest of America. And my driver Satan, whom you know well, will take you where everyone else is on the side of the road on their hands and knees waiting for my instructions. Now Scooooowt, before I get even more angry with you.

Ok Mark, you ready for this? I think you'll get a kick out of this one. It's time to leave you and everyone for the time being. But before I go, I need to make one more call on this demonic device that my next-door neighbor invented. Then after that I will send an email out to all mankind. I think they call this Spam. Where did these people come up with these words? You got me, Jesus, anyway. I just want to thank you Mark my son for being such a faithful servant to me. You heard the call and you listened. Not like all the people I am going to call now. But wait Lord, you can't leave yet. There are still many others you need to call to account. Yes, I know Mark. I'm not going anywhere yet, I was just showing you my gratitude for not falling back into this mess of society, even though I kept that thorn in your side. Like I said Mark, my strength works best in your weakness, Amen.

Real quick, What on earth were those evil billboards doing I saw hanging up all over New York City, Brooklyn and Queens the other day while I was driving around with you delivering parts? Just more lies from the devil. Well Jesus, from what it looks like to me, the devil hung every one of them. You can say that again, Mark, you can say that.

"Get Rich or Die Trying", Are these people serious Mark? What kind of movie is this? This is out of control I tell you, absolutely out of control. One big lie from my good old neighbor Satan, obviously. Hollywood, does not have the word, "Holy" in it. I think I will clean all that up next Mark and I will name it "Holy"wood. No more lies Mark, I have had it with these evil people looking to make money off of my gullible and naive children. No more. Now do me a favor Mark, after Satan drops off all the American mommies and daddies and children by the side of the road. Have him and all his little devil driver's head on out to Hollywood California with all those Hummer limos because I have got plenty of new passengers for him. Thank you Mark, no problem Jesus, my pleasure. Excuse me Lord, yes Mark, shall I have him make any stops along the way? Nope, that will be fine Mark. We got just about everybody so far I think. Just tell him to hurry because time is running out for America, okey-doke Jesus.

All right then, how shall I approach all these hotshot in Hollywood, Mark? Don ask me Jesus, that's a mess over there. How about you place an "Ark" like the one you had Noah build, on top of the Hollywood sign. Then have your father God, open up the skies with a rain like no other before seen. When all these huge mansions start getting washed away into the Pacific Ocean, you could then stand on the stern of your ship and show them who the real boss is. You're nuts Mark, let me tell you. I wonder about you sometimes. You're right Mark, I do need to find you a wife. I see it is starting to get to you, isn't it? Starting? C'mon Jesus, it's been playing on my brain for quite some time now. Yes, I know Mark. Just be thankful you never married any of those women that my next-door neighbor put in your path. You can say that again Lord, amen.

OK then, listen up Mr. and Mrs. movie star. Your time is up. And as for you, Mr. and Mrs movie producers. You should all be ashamed of yourselves for what you put on the big screen and little screen in America's homes. Since you never gave me a passing thought as you pranced around with all that arrogance and pride, I'm not gonna waste much time on you either.

For the few of you who acknowledged me, I want you to enter the doors on my ship. And the rest of view, head to the Hummers,' where my neighbor and his driver's await you. Now get! Disgusting I tell you, absolutely disgusting. Wow, look at em all Mark. Millions and millions, weeping on their hands and knees. Like it says in my book the Bible. A day when strong men, will cry bitterly. The time has come.

A billboard that has a guy pointing a gun at whoever is stupid enough to look it, and the name of the game is called, "True Crime" in big letters. Then" New York City", play the game. This must be one of those Nintendo games, ha Mark? Oh no Jesus, that's outdated. This is America, remember? We need something new every couple weeks. I think it's called X box. Notice the "X". More demonic names. People love evil Jesus. They buy it up. I never heard of crime, being true. It is all backwards like you said would happen, Jesus. Well this is no game, people of America, and your fun and games are over. Mark, yes Lord, you better tell me what ever is left on your mind my son, because you are heading up to heaven soon. Maybe not so for the majority of the rest of this country America. I "Jesus Christ", just want to tell every person who reads this book that My Buddy Mark here is not a communist and that he loves this country. By no means does he not appreciate the fact that he is blessed to live in America. He is just trying to warn the American public about the lies from my neighbor the devil. OK Jesus, this makes me sad Lord, I never wanted this day to come for all these people. What I have to say is meaningless compared to this scenario. Go ahead Mark,

Ok Jesus, real quick, getting back to the cell phone epidemic. Do you think maybe I'm just a little jealous that even if I owned one, the damn thing would not ring anyway? Nooooo Mark, you don't want any of these people calling you anyway. Oh okay, thanks, I was just curious. One more question Jesus and then I will leave you alone for a while. You see, that's just it Mark, I don't ever want you to leave me alone. I want my people to call on me constantly. I'm their only hope and I have every answer they will ever need to life's problems. Amen Jesus, Amen. I agree a hundred percent with you. OK then, last question for the time being. How come on eharmony dot com, the online dating site they only broadcast on their advertisements on the radio the testimonies of Fred and Wilma hitting it off on the first date and not the hundreds of thousands that have wasted not only their money but their precious time trying to find a mate? All part of the big lie Mark, it's called false advertisement. It's everywhere. Just like the beer commercials showing people who don't even drink beer holding one in their hand. Anything for them to make money.

America On Lies. I checked out that America on line while you were sleeping the other night Mark. You did Jesus? Yes, your right Mark, This is bad news my son. Constantly flashing new pictures and demonic stuff in my children's faces. Something like, America takes it off. People dancing and prancing around with hardly any clothes on. Talking about how "gay is in". This is sick, I must admit. Who is this Brad something and Angelina something? Do people really pay attention to people such as these Mark? I'm afraid so Lord. Amazing, absolutely amazing. This guy leaves his wife, for her, and no one even mentions this horrible part. I don't approve of this selfish uncaring behavior. I even put the television on the other night to Mark. "America Idol". This truly is a show that was produced my next door neighbor, Satan himself. I am the only Idol people should be worshipping. There is not much hope here for this country Mark, I am sorry to say my son. I can appreciate your president trying to help the people of Iraq. But I think he may be there for impure motives. Not that all people, don't deserve freedom. This life down here is only temporary. I am truly the only way to everlasting freedom, Praise God , Amen. I am the only God there is, not no human being. This president of yours is a little high on himself and the powers that America has given him. Not Good either, not good at all. While I am at it I want to call all Teachers of my father's word from far and wide. I see some of you have made my Father's house, "The Church", into a market place. Using the word of God for your own personal gain. Some of you have even fallin back into sin. You are a threat to my neighbor satan and that is why he attacks you so often. No excuse however. You put your hand to the plow and have fallen back to ungodly ways some of you, "And you know who you are". Now go and join everyone else by the curb on their hands and knees. Start to repent like everyone else and maybe I'll have mercy on you all.

1-1-06. Happy New Year Jesus, Same to you Mark. What did you do for new years Mark? That's not funny Jesus. You know exactly what I did. Just trying to have some fun with you Mark. Well it's not funny Jesus, I have just about had it. I have been acknowledging and seeking you for the last 8 to 9 years and I must admit this is no easy task at times. I am very lonely at times. Oh relax Mark, that's just my neighbor playing with your mind and emotions. From what I understand, you never had a wife or a girlfriend either Jesus. How did you deal with that all your 33 years on this earth? I am going to flip my lid soon Lord. I am a healthy guy, when you gonna send someone my way? In my time Mark, in my time not yours. Like I said before. So now for your question Mark, which is a very good one at that especially since I said it is not good for man to be alone. You see Mark, there are seasons for everything my son. Why don't you go open your Bible up and go to Ecclesiastes "3", "A time For Everything". And write this down in your little book you got going here. Maybe this will make you feel better today. And besides remember the great reward that awaits you in heaven. This world and everything in it is coming to an end as you know it. So relax my son and keep doing what I tell you. Yes Jesus, I hear you. Thanks for another lesson. As usual, a little painful for my flesh, yet nourishing for my spirit and soul, Amen.

"A time For Everything"
There is a time for everything,
a season for every activity under heaven.
A time to be born and a time to die.
A time to plant and a time to harvest.
A time to kill and a time to heal.
A time to tear down and a time to rebuild.
A time to cry and a time to laugh.
A time to grieve and a time to dance.
A time to scatter stones and a time to gather stones.
A time to embrace and a time to turn away.
A time to search and a time to lose.
A time to keep and a time to throw away.
A time to tear and a time to mend.
A time to be quiet and a time to speak up.
A time to love and a time to hate.
A time for war and a time for peace.

All right then Mark, how do you feel now, a little better? No, I don't Jesus. I want a loving christian wife and wanna know when your gonna send me one. You even said it Jesus. Tis not good for man to be alone. You hit the nail on the head with that comment Lord. Now listen hear Mark, you obviously did not get a good nights sleep again. Go back and read "A Time For Everything" and I bet this time around it will have a different effect on you, Ok buddy? Yes Jesus, no problem, sorry for my bad attitude. As you know, I am far from perfect. Just finish this book Mark. Warn this country like I asked you to. See you soon Mark. Wait, don't leave Jesus, I thought you said you had one more phone call and email to send out. Not to worry Mark, In just a little time, you will be with me again. I will let America remain on their hands and knees where they should have been once in a while any way. (Jeremiah 29:11). "For I know the plans I have for you,"says the Lord. "They are plans for good and not for disaster, to give you a future and a hope.

Ok than, America, time is up. Are you going to invite me into your lives or do you want to go to Hell, forever and ever? Tick, tick, tick, tick, tick, tick, clock is ticking, its now or never.

Beep, Beep, Beep, Beep, Beep,Beep,. We interrupt this broadcast, for, "This was only a test". We repeat, "This was only a test". If Jesus Christ really had come back, this broadcast would not have even made it to your ears. So repent now and let the Lord into your heart before it is to late. Because when he comes back, your time will be up. No second chances. Those who wait till the Eleventh hour to know Jesus Christ, will die at ten o'clock. So I beg of you to seek him now, Praise God, Amen.

All right then America. I hope you enjoyed that little possible consequence when the Lord comes back. Don't let this country, "America" program you. You program your self, Amen. This will not be easy for evil is every where. America on line already owns americaonlies.com and america-onlies.net. So I will put up americaonlies.org, I repeat in capital letters

AMERICAONLIES.ORG. Hopefully, I can make a difference in this country and start sending out the truth. As usual, I will put some scripture from the Bible at the end, for those of you who are interested. Please read on. I thank you for your precious time,

Sincerely, Mark Cullin, Praise God, Amen.

(2 Timothy 1:3-4) Timothy (you the reader my new friend), I thank God for you. He is the God I serve with a clear conscience, just as my ancestors did. Night and day I constantly remember you in my prayers. I'll long to see you again, for I remember your tears as we parted. And I will be filled with joy when we are together again.

(Romans I: 10-12) One of the things I always pray for is the opportunity, God willing, to come at last to see you. For I long to visit you so I can share a spiritual blessing with you that will help you grow strongly in the Lord. I'm eager to encourage you in your faith, but I also want to be encouraged by yours. In this way, each of us will be a blessing to the other.

(Romans I: 28-32) When they refused to would knowledge God, he abandoned them to their evil lines and let them do things that should never be done. Their lives became full of every kind of wickedness, sin, greed, hate, envy, murder, fighting, the exception, malicious behavior, and gossip. They are back steppers, haters of God, insolent, proud and boastful. They are forever inventing new ways of sinning and are disobedient to their parents. They refuse to understand, break their promises, and are heartless and unforgiving. They are fully aware of God's death penalty for those who do these things, yet they go right ahead and do them anyway. And, worse yet, they encourage others to do them, too.

(Romans I-18:24) But God shows his anger from heaven against all sinful, wicked people who push the truth away from themselves. For the truth about God is known to them instinctively. God has put this knowledge in their hearts. From the time the world was created, people have seen the earth and sky and all that God made. They can clearly see his invisible qualities—his eternal power and divine nature. So they have no excuse whatsoever for not knowing God. Yes, they knew God, but they wouldn't worship him as God or even give him banks. And they began to think up foolish ideas of what God was like. The result was that their minds became dark and confused. Claiming to be wise, they became utter fools instead. And instead of worshiping the glorious, ever-living God, they worshiped idols made to look like mere people, or birds and animals and snakes. So God let them go ahead and do what ever shameful things their hearts desired.

(Acts 28: 26-27) Go and say to my people, you will hear my words, but you will not understand; You will see what I do, but you will not perceive its meaning. For the hearts of these people are hardened, and their ears cannot hear, and they have closed their eyes—so there eyes cannot see, and their ears cannot hear, and their hearts cannot understand, "And they cannot turn to me and let me heal them".

(Isaiah 66: 2-3) My hands have made both heaven and earth, and they are mine. I, the Lord, have spoken! and " I will bless those who have humble and a contrite hearts, who tremble at my word. But those who choose their own ways, delighting courthouse in their sins, are cursed.

(Jeremiah 29: 11-14) "For I know the plans a have for you, says the Lord. " They are plans for good and not for disaster, to give you a future and a hope." In those days when you pray, I will listen. If you look for me in earnest, you will find me when you seek me. I will be found by you, says the Lord.

In times of deep trouble, it may appear as though God has forgotten you. But God may be preparing you, as he did the people of Judah for a new beginning with him.

(Daniel 10-12) Don't be afraid, Daniel. Since the first day you began to pray for understanding and to humble yourself before your God, your request has been heard in heaven. I have come in answer to your prayer.

(Acts 2:25-28) ' I know the Lord is always with me. I will not be shaken, for he is right beside me. No wonder my heart is filled with joy, and my mouth shouts his praises! my body rests in hope. For you will not leave my soul among the dead or allow your Holy one to rot in the grave. You have shown me the way of life, and you will give me wonderful joy in your presence.

40—" Save yourselves from this generation that has gone astray!"

(Acts 13-38:39) ' Brothers, listen! in this man Jesus there is forgiveness for your sins. Everyone who believes in him is freed from all guilt and declared right with God.

(2 Corinthians 5:17) What this means is that those who become Christians become new persons. They are not the same anymore, for the old life is gone. A new life has begun!

When people become Christians, their entire life changes. This doesn't mean that they dress differently, drive a new car, or change their hair style. Rather, it means that the new believers are cleansed of their sins and given a new reason for a living. They also begin to look at life from God's perspective. Everything changes—from how they treat an enemy to how they spend money. If you are a Christian, you could look forward to God making some exciting changes in your life. Be open to the changes, God wants to make in you. You won't regret it in the end.

(Galatians 5:16-26) "Living by the Spirit's Power". So I advise you to live according to your new life in the Holy Spirit. Then you won't be doing what your sinful nature craves. The old sinful nature loves to do evil, which is just opposite from what the Holy Spirit wants. And the Spirit gives us desires that are opposite from what the sinful nature desires. These two forces are constantly fighting each other, and your choices are never free from this conflict. But when you were directed by the holy spirit, you are no longer subject to the law.

When you follow the desires of your sinful nature, your life will produce these evil results: sexual immorality, impure thoughts, eagerness for lustful pleasure, idolatry, participation in demonic activities, hostility, quarreling, jealousy, outbursts of anger, selfish ambition, divisions, the feeling that everyone is wrong except those in your own little group, envy, drunkenness, wild parties, and other kinds of sin. let me tell you again, as I have before, that anyone living that sort of life will not inherit the kingdom of God.

But when the Holy Spirit controls our lives, he will produce this kind of fruit in us: love, joy, peace, patience, kindness, goodness, faithfulness, gentleness, and self control. Here there is no conflict with the law. Those who belong to Christ Jesus have nailed the passions and desires of their sinful nature to his cross and crucified them there. If we're living now but the Holy Spirit, let us follow the Holy spirit's leading in every part of our lives. Let us not become conceited, or irritate one another, or be jealous of one another.

(Galatians 6) "We Reap What We Sow". Dear brothers and sisters, if another Christian is overcome by some sin, you who are godly should gently and humbly help that person back on to the right path. And be careful not to fall into the same temptation yourself. Share each others' troubles and problems, and in this way obey the Lord Christ. If you think your too important to help someone in need, your only fooling yourself. You are really a nobody. Don't be misled. Remember that you can't ignore God and get away with it. You will always reap what you sow! Those who live only to satisfy their own sinful desires will harvest the consequences of decay and death. But those who live to please the Spirit will harvest everlasting life from the Spirit. So don't get tired of doing what is good. Don't get discouraged and give up, for we will reap a harvest of blessing at the appropriate time. Whenever we have the opportunity, we should do good to everyone, especially toward our Christian brothers and sisters.

(Ephesians) If you honor your father and mother, " you will live a long life, full of blessing."

(Peter 3) "Suffering for Doing Good" Remember, it is better to suffer for doing Good, if that is what God wants, than to suffer for doing wrong!

(Thessalonians 5: 16-18) Always be joyful. Keep on praying. No matter what happens, always be thankful, for this is God's will for you who belong to Christ Jesus. We might wonder how someone can rejoice or be joyful all the time, especially during painful or difficult experiences. But unlike happiness, which is based on circumstances, joy is a positive and confident outlook on life, despite our circumstances. Knowing that God is in control and that his love surrounds us gives us security and confidence. No matter what happens, we should delight in God and praise him for his goodness.

(Luke 11: 9-10) And so I tell you, keep on asking, and you will be given what you ask for. Keep on looking, and you will find. Keep on knocking, and the door will be opened. For everyone who asks, receives. Everyone who seeks, finds. And the door is open to everyone who knocks.

(Colossians 3: 12-15) "Living The New Life" Since God chose you to be the holy people whom he loves, you must cloth yourselves with tender hearted mercy, humility, cheerfulness, and patience. You must make allowance for each other's faults and forgive the person who offends you. Remember, the Lord forgave you, so you must forgive others. And the most important piece of clothing you must wear is "Love". Love is what binds us all together in perfect harmony. And let the peace that comes from Christ rule in your hearts.

(I Corinthians 13: 4-8) Love is patient and kind. Love is not jealous or boastful or proud or rude. Love does not demand its own way. Love is not irritable, and it keeps no record of when it has been wronged. It is never glad about injustice but rejoices whenever the truth wins out. Love never gives up, never loses faith, is always hopeful, and endures through every circumstance.

Well my friends. I wish I could put the whole Bible in here for you. Please get a New Living Translation Bible for your self, one day if you could. Once again thank you very much for you time and I will speak with all of you again, one day soon.

May the Lord bless you all, once again. Sincerely, with Love, Your buddy, Mark

P.S. I dedicate this book to every American citizen. We don't realize how blessed we are to live in this country. Some of us do, I imagine. We should acknowledge God each and every day we are alive and live in this beautiful land of ours. Amen.

Well folks what's it gonna be??? You gonna keep buying into this Big Lie or what??? I hope not. Come join me and make a difference in this country that God gave us. Maybe there is hope for America yet.

Thanks for your precious time and don't let technology ruin your life. "If you don't program yourself, then America will program you.

Sincerely, Mark Cullin

AMERICAONLIES.ORG